LITTLE QUAKES EVERY DAY

Caroline Hardaker was born in the North East in 1986, and has lived there ever since, mostly in Newcastle. Her poetry has been read live on BBC Radio and published in numerous anthologies and magazines, including *Magma*, *The Interpreters House*, *Shoreline of Infinity*, and in anthologies from The Emma Press. When she's not writing poetry, she's also a novelist, occasional librettist, and fibre artist – her sculptures have been sold to collectors around the world. You'll normally see her carrying a backpack, just in case she's swept off on an adventure.

Caroline's debut pamphlet, *Bone Ovation*, was published by Valley Press in 2017. Her debut novel, *Composite Creatures*, will be published in May 2021 (Angry Robot Books).

Little Quakes Every Day

Caroline Hardaker

Valley Press

First published in 2020 by Valley Press
Woodend, The Crescent, Scarborough, YO11 2PW
www.valleypressuk.com

ISBN 978-1-912436-46-0
Cat. no. VP0166

A CIP record for this book is available from the British Library.

Cover design by Jamie McGarry.
Cover illustration by Ben Hardaker.
Text design by Peter Barnfather.
Edited by Jo Brandon.

Printed and bound in Great Britain by
Imprint Digital, Upton Pyne, Exeter.

Contents

INVENTIONS

To Ben,

For patiently listening to lots of lines that don't make a lot of sense until strung together later (a bit like life really), for teaching me history every day, and for inspiring my sense of discovery.

These poems are for you.

contemplate
—SPACE—
and the breaths
between

stars
particles
and the spark
that ignites in your eye

at the sighting
of even the

littlest find

PART ONE

Histories

Even buried giants
rumble, groan in their sleep,
and dream dreams
of daylight

On Polar Bears Brought Together by the Death of a Humpback Whale

The boulders approach, grown with hoary turf
and smudging rune-marks across the tundra;
a moving tide to mount the hunt that's found.
Jaws meet meat in many places to break the hide.

In the belly, brothers do not know brothers;
skins smell of sleep, birth-blood lost, and the beasts
take turns to tear out the swim-bladder or fists
of blubber. The bears are tied together with ropes

of knotted gut, and each hollows out his grotto
from fat, oiling his coat as if preparing for battle in woad –
but white as snow. Drifts of broad backs reinvent genesis.
Slow stomachfuls last a day, a night, a day,

and pressing for the last, boulders roll in the colossal arch;
ribs hanging above like paths of comets. After the feast,
blood flecks the ice like constellations, and then,
stones in a round, each brother licks his sores and retreats alone.

The supernova shatters, and the whale shrinks.

A Portrait on a House-Skin

The house-skins are brushed with a master's precision,
in a portrait of a greater house, *the horizon*.
One belly of a room becomes the sun;
the earthworm curves of peripheral hills,
the humps of still hips – a family together,
and the ink of moon dripping on a mud flat.

All of this painted in stained glass, cross-hatched
by drinn-grass dropped from the back of a pack mule,
the mule's hoof-prints, flecks of sand-shine
in sandals. A gap in the face of it –
a dark cartouche rimmed with lips of grey clay
and humming a truth drawn in harlequins,
the facets cut and polished to turn a rock to ruby.

A cow plods out of this mouth
and leans on one illustrated wall
as a sister would on her sister after a deep sharing.
Her body full of song, heavy with cream,
arms around shoulder-ridges like children.

Glyptodon Terraces

We dwell in a belly that walked from winter.

Rain attacks a roof sketched with miles like the rings
inside a tree's gut, cut with interlocking dog-daisies
that follow the sun's offerings above my children.

Before and after them, this room pulses with moving parts;
kin in curls like upturned lice, to replace a pumping heart
and four claws that folded grasslands. On waking,
I watch the rising white through a notch
just the width to poke a finger through –
or a spear.

Behind the rear arch are planted two smaller domes
as if following the first. The roof edges are plugged bluntly
to the mud flats, and are so very still,
but stirring within
as if dreaming.

Pterosaur

for Mary Anning, b.1799 – d.1847

On a quaint and cold English coast
she perches in briny shallows; a pink flamingo
in a sea of *how do you do*, and *thank you*,
pocketing cockle shells, mermaid's purses,
aery foreign bodies and forgotten peculiarities. An ammonite;
soon to be mounted in a lady's pendant, brachiopods;
fringed with shallow ridges, lashes fanned like moth's wings,
a crown of preserved coral; a scrying dome for thinker's-fortunes,
and pale opalescent starfish; peaked with bestial spines
to be dried later on taut strings in bright sunlight.
Hundreds of lucky purse-pearls for travelers,
bone-tokens and runes. Treasures to frame a window seat
and chime inside pouches,
making empty quarters sing.

Worlds are birthed from cold clods of earth.

Thumbs in the abdomen, she learns through slow labours
how to empty chalk downs for bronze or the heady-flush
of blood-rust. How to tease apart coprolite husks
to comprehend habit. One stone flint lives in her fist,
but she is gentle with it
so as not to break sensibility.

Mary stands with one foot in a shallow grave.

On the white cliffs, with brush and a scalpel whet on scorn –
she is emissary to the first albatross and its mechanics,
leather swathes, and greatsword at each wrist.
Listen, its dead voice erupts from an old moon,
mounted between the eyes. She counts the rods, pillars,
columns, mapping architecture to blueprint the future of flight.

But then, digging deeper, there –

(a truth entombed until the work is disclosed)
a clutch of eggs, bound in a dead cloud.
A dozen ossified promises
ended before a new world could meet them.

Picea Abies
[one Norway spruce]

stalk stick
water up the chalk
and bone
yellow cumber wet and warm
a white dog on the lawn
and t a n g of golden piss

watch

the crown of ticklers up top
moonnut *cracks* andskinandwing
come out

sometimes fall
[bump]
then hollow

sad crumble bush

no more roarandrush
of fir
brush
on
brush
little gems *[ting]* single quick

roselight and glintysquint

over lovers shhhhh c u d d l i n g
cutting
with sharp mineral *thing*

seepbloodsap and s c a r

proddypeopletwigs
in holes squeaking at leggy creepers
then they go

cold and frost coming

Shepherd's Delight

Neck incurved like a bare cream moon –
the heifer bellows a weary *huff*
worthy of a day's trudging.

Crown bowed, she takes her seat
beneath a new cloud;
freshly formed, pink, and rising,
rounded like a bell, a cowslip,
or a full udder's teat.

Over the Fence

"Aye, a na, he is a pig
but he's also a king as well
with grand argyll wings
and eyes like a canny harlequin,
makin me laugh,
and mesmerising my interiors.
All lies, a na,
but butter-softened,
sweet and tasty
on the tip of me tongue, even
when it's acid-spittin.

Aye, a na, a na,

he's won,
but his sugar postpartum
is worth a king's ransom
n any argyll leathers he fancies havin.
N look at him,
he's handsome."

Afternoon Tea with the Millers

Thomas Edison taught his second wife to speak Morse code so they could secretly communicate by tapping on each other's arms whilst in company.

My dear, days like today remind me that I'm glad I married you
and not your family.
I am the fox in the farmyard, drinking the dairy's sour milk
under the dim gaze of the slow-cow, seated betwixt juvenile pigs
squinting in monocles and pernickety hens
stuffed into lace dresses,
pecking at yesterday's conversational crumbs.

It's been more than three hours now, and I can hardly bear
to listen another moment to your mother's clucking
or your father's crowing. All feathers and bluster,
without a speck of doing around this idle table;
sat with defiantly single, unfitting cogs.
Note how your father fondles his moustache
with a fancy for his own words;
always land-locked concepts looping.
He sets off on a venture only to return to the same end
as before, but in another guise, wearing another hat.
Still, always the same upturn of his nose

and bellows that I can't fathom through that haystack beard.
See how his eyes flick between you and I
and your cousins for a rise, or a smile
often at my own expense;

Ho! He says. *It's enough to give an ideas-man ideas!*

I play the clam-ear here, preferring to feign isolation
than to lie outright. Oh, the flame is lit inside
and it's a wonder my ears aren't smoking.
See how your mother tuts at my finger-tick?

Poor over-affectionate Edison! You've addled his brain, Mina,
he touches you insistently. The muse has made of him a mute!

Perhaps I would reply, if the tea (dry as tinder)
didn't stick so on the fox-throat which longs to swallow them whole.

Thank God for bare wrists, Mina.
I hope you're picking all this up over their squawking,
your soft head-nods and kind-hearted purrs.
Tell them sweetly, feline, that I don't speak goose.

The Puppeteer

I. THINKING

Standing in the prologue, he thinks in the third act –
the steps between misplaced before they're made.
Muscles move within inert limbs to dance the wooden body,
and twinning wakes
the sleeping space between control bar and crown –
up and down, up and down,
little lives spanned by strings.

II. PLAYING

His hair on cheek is silk on silk,
and runs like rain on wood, as straight as sleet.
Her shadow is his face, is an eclipse
as painted eyes rise to the lamps, little sculpted hands
cupped to hold his soul below, white as caster sugar
and wrapped in what he'd sewn for her.
A ruff from a tattered glove, hem from twisted antique lace
and a patchwork bodice stitched from his own hose,
darned each moon, worn raw from the waltz.
His toes curl defunct on wasted soles.

III. ENCORE

Her toes tap the wood with a *crack, crack, crack*
beneath pillars, columns of law, and strings
that play a low note – always one of woe. He is cello,
she is viola. Skyward cuff-buckles are Saturn's rings,
and coughs and claps punch through like stars, comets,
a flaming meteor in the lights down.
Their bow conducts applause, such wooden clapping
oak on oak – a rose with many thorns. They stand
in the light as one, and time falls again like rain.

The Great Massarti goes into Liquidation

On 3rd January 1872, Massarti (Thomas Macarte) was performing with Manders' Menagerie in Bolton, England when he was attacked by four lions in his act. The lion tamer was killed in front of several hundred onlookers.

In the news:
'Sons in plot to supplant father from family business.
The household lies in disarray, their father in pieces.'

* * *

"I am a giant, chained under the shadow of a weak skin-strip
armed with a wooden chair and whip. My pedestal
stands atop my cage. At my call, I will pull the cord in my jaws –
bringing down the velvet on Massarti's neck."

"I hear you brother, and taste the rise of murder
on the licks of our father's fire-wheel. His stump smells
of pulled muscles and triumph. I'll leap through the rings of rib
to hunt the heart. His talent will linger long on my lips."

"Oh – lustful blood and skillful execution! I will hold his hip
in service to my brothers. Allow me to eat the bowel,
and I will step down to the wings when the time comes;
Massarti's belly in my belly, an echo on an echo."

"My brothers; I love my father, but I love you more.
I am the dancer far upstage, eyes to the clicking of your clogs
while mine mis-step, a second slower. I will take Massarti's mane
for my own, limp puppet-strings and manhood on which to graze."

Testimony of a Witch to Hang: 1614

If it's my fancy to wish for you,
consult the moon in quiet,
or to cut a stem with the intention
of prolonging its bloom –
is that witchery, too?

Why have my doings plagued you
with such gloom? They're all for hope of a curing.
All my giving – to curve the flow of a world
weighted with its own doom, while men
and children sit and wait for fate to finish them.
Thin hands pressed, their fledgling eyes
closed against the end, sores unclothed –
I soar and mount the air

and know this;
I've sown a part of me in all of you, a gift –
the seed of guilt. Once I'm strung a-drop,
I'll grow anew, in you
as fear and regret,
your reasoning lost, beset with woe,
and every mother-tree will remind you
of me, this courtroom,
and the words I swore in front of you all.

Libulan reads the sage smoke for an answer

In Filipino mythology, Libulan is frequently portrayed as a 'two spirit' divinity, and is revered for prophesies and shaman-like abilities.

What is it that gnaws at your throat? Is it a sickness of the soul? Your eyes are the strangest blue – as a dead limb chills, or a weary sea longs for shore with no moon-wrench to summon it home. Is a part of you trapped out there amidst the seven lights, grasping for a hand? I have had long enough with my own thoughts, *the echo*, to know the tremble of a bowl ringing. Are you coming back already, without my poultice? Who are you? Did your mother murmur in your cradle that we're all both sun and shadow, the gentle curve of a brass bell and the clashing gong? When did your singing die? If our necks met like dried roots they might kiss. *Hush.* Sometimes, the brightest things are crushed by light. See these hands, bones and copper, flat on the wood pyre? They slice pigs to read the twists, then cradle stones that could be hearts. And they weep. Do you want to be someone else? Are you shackled to where you've been, kneeling with a woven moss-mantle upon you? Are you disappearing into what you've done? Your eyes are the strangest blue – like a face in the lake or cold lips and the fingers grasping your throat are shaking.

Siddhārtha hears a song performed by a travelling musician

Reputedly born in Ancient Nepal, Prince Siddhārtha grew up sheltered from suffering until he chose to leave his palace. After years of inner searching, he became the Buddha.

My Prince, your eye. It carries the look of the wolf –
while the sun is here, with me, carried between us in the cradle
(it happens today then, that light)

It is that song, Yaśodharā. It catches the tail of the dove that sleeps
perched on my rib, and awake he quivers, eyes open

It is a mountain song, breathing cold loneliness into the palace.
Of places where rain is rain, not lotus blossoms birthing falling flowers
(it takes him there, a hoopoe tethered to a stone)

Such blue and cold calling – it chills the fingers. I think such falls exist here
in secret. One night, I held out my tongue to be a crow

The world is wide, my love. I hear it's the twisting of the red parts inside,
the heavy falling of water, suffering, and dust on dust on dust
(my homeland is forest and fruit and it cries for me)

What is suffering, wife? Is it the sad lamp of the moon?
Maybe I, burning brighter, could remedy that white face

But we sit on the sun, husband. Pain is separation. Pain is the apple's pip.
A bird with plucked feathers. Coal in the gold. Ill weather on the sea
(please, plant your talons in my joy and hold tight)

The song is a question. It makes me look up
then down into my hands. All is inside a bowl and upside-down

Sit down, Siddhārtha. The walls are loud. Red flowers, and the floor roars
like water and is speckled with pyrite. It glitters, but bites
(the guards see him, are singing, are swinging their cups to him)

No. It tastes like tomorrow and the inbreath of the king in quiet,
the hang after a fall. I will taste the bitter fruit, Yaśodharā, to know the sweet

Kiss your son, then, who still sups milk from me
and in seven early days has already learned solitude
(go, and when you turn, you will see silver shatter into rain)

Ahalya

In Hindu mythology, Ahalya is a complex character. She is often portrayed as a victim, her destiny a consequence of the actions of the men she knew. This is not necessarily true.

Ever cupped tight by hands, not born of dark parts, made of light
then married to hunger and empty space on a husband's spoon.
Is this all? A face up in cold rain, and he calls me his 'mynah', but
in the hour when the sky weeps, I pray to the parakeet

for a monsoon. And then, *imagine it*, a feast. Lifted on the back
of a wild crane without weight and spread across his wings,
rubies drip down my throat and *I tasted me* – plums and apricots.
Moon milk. The white lotus. Honey from an ungraspable sack of bees.

This was my precious night of sweet fruits and light

but I was cut to pieces, cast down in the pit of fire for *knowing*,
made a grey stone to his eye. But I still have a tongue,
and tell the garden a truth that summons thunder – that I'll rise
at the brush of a stranger's toe, a cracked heel on my back.

Gloria, Hag

An antique bookshop revealed to me a note,
folded between the pages of a rotting botany tome.

Together with a preserved marigold was pressed a prayer –
ink-dripped, and marked with the sign of a helical worm and star.

* * *

Hag, Gloria-Hag,
where have you been since Samhain?
Sleeping, the glue betwixt the rocks and lichen
perhaps, or lifted on a lick of flame,

in some stone hearth? Would you be
listening low to the pleasure groans from homes
down hamlet ways, all doors to us closed, below?
Where, where did you go?

Which form did you choose, Gloria, to wear?
The earthenware rat? The horned ram of grasses,
or the buzzard? The hunt-jump from sky to soil
is worth the pain of a transformation.

What did you hear, Gloria, while a child-cat of the world?
Converge with us twelve here, again, in worm-form,
skin sticking in sacred mud and we'll debate what needs done.
We will make of ourselves a root-knot

until the setting sun sets the hares to rest
and coats our skins with the night's frost. Then,
the bear will rise, and white the stone over our Mother's
buried bones. This is where I will wait for you –

holding a fox pelt to welcome you home,
back to our sisters, all ears turned to you, all grown.

The Morrígan Meets a Lover on the Battlefield

In Irish mythology, the Morrígan is a shape-shifting goddess of war.

We are a black arrow above war, compass west, a slash of moon
and jagged flapping, like a hinged wooden thing hunting wet and red iron
in the rain. *There!* We crow dive and are in the mud, grasping the axe

with your eyes in our mouth. But *soft, soft*; we melt like wax in the lamplight
of your face. Oh, bright one with flickering heart – we dream less prophetic dreams
after we eat. But why are your pockets so full of feathers, why does your woman

wear an oily plume in her coat? Did you know, child, that winged and over water
we're reborn – not once, but twice? Not you. You're already gone. So rise, thief –
it snows on the fells and the wild mare runs like thunder, anger, dread.

Medusa

I wasn't there, but I'm accused of arson.
"It was Medusa. She sparked the match."
I'm not my own, my mane – a sunflower, stalked
from behind as I follow the moon. A stem bending
sensuously, smooth as slithering glass.
Stare enough, and you'll see two eyes in the back of my head.
Dank, sad pebbles sunken to the bottom of a pool.
You snicker. It's all a bit of fun –
bumping thumbs down there, a lick with a leather tongue
and a kiss like a flute pressed hard on the lips.

I hide within the tangled knots of song,
palms flat to my thighs and scaled to the wrist with
skin itching to shed. All the time,
you say it's *me* that lit your embers,
shut you down, turned the softer part of you to stone.

Bean-Nighe

A shadow raps at her door and leaves a bundle
of cloth to wash on the step. Some, the quiet all-colour
of skin, melancholic baby-faded shades within the weight
of grey and night-black. Without a word, she's gone

before being there. The washerwoman ties the bundle
to her bones with sea-rope and scrubs out what's writ;
breaking the weave on the great stone's back.
By dawn, the sea is braided with blood, and she returns

for the fare she's earned, knocking at doors,
waiting still as milk – but few doors open
to take in their shrouds. *Why? Why?* she cries.
Take them. Take them. Take them.

Loss

Blood was the balm, my kiss;
holding on like red anemones. Cocoon.
Keep warm and burrow, little rabbit.
Hot soil cups the sun's every curve –
balance the little ball.

But the grip goes. She's gone, and
night-dark drops to swallow the light.
She's old iron, in my hands, alone,
in pieces, like rose petals
drying.

PART TWO

Discoveries

so they thrust up, oaks
to judge the wild stuff;
ghosts and mauve roots and smoke,
mouths full of their own fruit

Taxonomical Divergences in Madagascar

Fifty-nine forms of the chameleon shift skins.
The transitioning split further, into sub-species
that grow adjacent, in diagonals.

At sight of a similarity, their chromatophores react
and strum the arms of stars, laid in lattice like stacks
of harps, playing against what they see,
a warning to themselves.

These low, plucking droplets sound under smiles
and a tuning-fork strike
erupts chaos of light. A newborn is thrust
through the split crust of earth,
where miles of plates move
in little quakes every day.

Stickleback

Sticklebacks in Switzerland have been observed evolving into two distinct species within the same lake.

Imagine that we are sticklebacks.

The pond is heavy, but innocent.
Our pockets are sewn closed, definite with stones,
and we're up to the hips in things that act dead.

A life in still water gives you time to think.

The pond is a portrait of a stream.
We're on the gallery bench, floating on our backs
with arms and legs spread like sea stars

when a bone in my spine snaps, and

the pond becomes a projection. A film on the wall.
I turn and say to you; *if I spread my fins*
and swim the stream –
will you think I don't exist?

Sproutling

I observed a wee sprout as I sat on the curb
(cheap sarnie in hand, contemplating the world)
rising from street ruins, ciggie butts and grit,
felted green shields rosing around a florid, raw-headed bud
bold and stark cerise,
flamboyantly blooming a-top a stalk already broken
by the swing of a lumbering boot.

Such a brave little bugger,
still growing despite its own end looming.

And here's to lots and lots of days

for Holly

There aren't any rules to this.
You have to make your own,
paint the world the colour of your eyes.
But know this, one thing is certain –
every day is an invention.
You're growing always, now,
upwards and away and back again,
your home a boat on a swaying lake
of many days.

There will be days when people will try
to change your mind. Plant those toes
in wet sand, permit the tide to move pebbles,
upturn shipwrecks (ripe for plunder with those you love)
and deposit all the sea's sunken treasures at your feet.
Pick up the shining nuggets that fit your pockets,
and let the ocean keep the rest for today.
There will be many tides and many treasures,
no one is keeping score.

There will be days when your head is full of learning
from the way older folk speak.
Your words will sound different to theirs
and umpteen voices will talk in a tangle
in your head. Fight it out in the concept-jungle,
cape tied around your neck,
sceptre poised in your hand.
Let what settles like moss on a stone, win.

There will be days when you don't know what
you're supposed to do. Be the face of a clock
which rotates in full twice a day
and is never wearing the same expression when it says 'hello'.
Enact little acts of kindness in every place.
These are your true petals, which bloom
no matter what colours you're wearing.
These are easy gifts from you to the world.

There will be days when all you want to do is run,
spread fledgling wings and take in more air
through your mouth than you ever have before.
To eat the world in utter freedom, alone,
your voice louder than all the buzzing below.
Let it happen, shout at the sky and
bellow out a tune like the most tone-deaf contralto.
Show the world the marvelous plumes
you've grown and which make you, you

because home will be there
when you need to tuck your head beneath your wing,
preen and groom a broken feather or two.
There will be days when a pair of warm arms
is the whole world
and the only true slumber is sleeping within them.
Become a love-knot, only untying
when the time is right – with a gentle tug.
There's no rush, a tight hug can stop time
while you prepare for tomorrow's adventure,
another day altogether.

Pebble

Clean, close
sweep, (clunk)
                    sweep!
Then blown a bit, held, pushed to chime with other
fellows, hugging under mellow ripples.
What joy, and skyward –
                    flickers of yellow!

That swifts by, tight black arrives,
and nymphs lick, tickle us;
(oh how we giggle)
and maybe even –
                    a little fish!

All drifting bits, all story, stars;
every round is a fresh delight,
such shows, sounds, and flickers of light.

On Opening a Love Note Delivered by Snail

I might just be a simple mushroom, bruised by weathers
and tipped by gloom, but you're one too (though far more moon-like).
I've heard you pulse your hyphae-strings many times,
tripping out a melody for my 'shroomy ears to hear.
I sang back every night to your fruiting body, gills rippling.
You've been eyeing me too, lifting up your pearl skirt
a little further each day, you flirt.

You don't belong in that distant dirt. Look over this deciduous lap
and see – I'm dipping my cap to you. It's taken me two weeks
to twist my stem down and around –
I'm sponge, and open to any crushing boot to stamp your way.
I'd choose to be the one broken in two,
if it gave you an extra day.

Listen, if we *both* move, migrate, we can start our patch
in half the time! Picture the young spores we'll have –
little meteorites, throbbing mycelium love notes like stars
to illuminate our wilting days. They might inherit your egg-shine,
or the convex of my cap. They'll bulb up, all clean, and we'll rub
up the cusps of each other until we stick, blunting memory-smudges
of where we've been, the underneaths only we've seen,
all raw ribs.

I can't wait to metabolise matter with you, consume a legume or two.
We can be casual at first, bloom, and then shrink under tented matters
as we feed our buttoned galley, *the family*.
I get softer with age, so be tender with me. I take in the sun
through a skinless skull. Consider this sensitivity when you respond.
Send the messenger snail back forthwith, with your answer –
he's not the quickest, you know,
and for us time is of the essence.

An Ant on Trial
and the Subsequent Dialogue

[As to the Leaf:]
Great teeth –
carrier of cadavers; quarter me,
oh bringer of scythes.

[Followed by the Aphid:]
Mother, feeder, leader, lover,
coaxer, mixer; stroke my back
for honey dew, milk. I know you.

[The Sparrow spoke:]
Tit-bit. Flicking morsel
a bite of red and bitterness. Quick –
find a hundred by the hill, the little clamps pinch.

[The domestic Cat:]
A plaything... little little darting thing.
Cover, paws over, *there you are!* Uncover, repeat –
eat. Empty. Look for another. Look at feet.

[Man:]
Thwarted, thieves of sweet meats.
Self-blame, shame, spilt sugar fields.
Medicate, sanitate, spray. Wipe away remains.

[And the Earth concluded:]
Swarm, oh pores.
Billions in capillaries, ground's marrow.
First and last. Conquerors.

Monkey Necks

Crafted to shackle a staggering ankle,
I am the lump in the swallow,
the drugged-lurch, the mash of brain on skull.
Yank me back and I cleave a shrill-shriek in two.
My captive's call cuts glass.

Closer than my keeper's family-tree –
my snaking dance gifts shoes to little feet. Throat-blood
from fathers and sons wrinkles in my links,
but skyward glittering eyes only grasp
the empty streets where the flakes gather.

I don't sing for them anymore, clammed-up
with the coin-taste and bitter-weight
of rust. I try to 'clink'
but manage just the scrape of iron on dust
through mud, a dull whimper.

It isn't yet winter

but all I hold is desiccated bark, retreating to cured origins.
Looking up through heavy roots, stems, wilted ends
I scope the sky; a life ponderous as slate
and prone to cracking at each new quake.
At every thought, sticks fall from their bundle.

All buds have blossomed and dropped,
leaving hollow cups and sham-caskets behind.
Stalks are splinters, tools to pen peculiar notes
woven in marrow odorous with iron-rust,
and which can only be read from the inside, out.

I am a rawhide diary;
my ink's black fading hand-in-hand
in sympathy with its ciphers.
Your face – a folded settlement to live in,
and between the leaves, a vestige of me, is recorded;
mouth frozen open
in a wide 'O'
of surprise.

Sun Burn

I very much wanted to reach it –
that pillar, alarm red with gaping gurn
shining with the postman's mark,

but my feet didn't quite work
and the sky inlaid with doom was dark.
I couldn't cognate the way to walk,

my legs were string, unravelling rope,
falling away in bits, post sulphur soak.
My fringing clothes didn't even fit me

and draped like an aged net curtain would,
my hairs split twigs from a starving tree.
All I wanted was to reach it, touch it even,

be electrified by this mast of men
stretching calls between continents.
A beacon of the street's love-ins and brawls.

In the end I couldn't, white blacked my eyes.
What if I was to not see the floor and fall,
contracting toxoplasmosis from cat-marked curbs?

It's not worth the risk. I insist, let the letter
yellow and knotted mind flow to remote suburbs
or further, to temperate sand-washed outskirts, just me –

not fraught at the thought of spores, or sepsis,
sharp birds in flight, or penetrating company.

Cicada

That song –
listen, hear the locusts tick? It brings to mind
a foreign clock marking a stint
while you've nothing to do but wait in winter,
spring burning away with every shiver.
It's even faster than those frittered seconds,
each snap pricking with flaky mortality.
This obvious applause for decay riles my insides –
it's almost encouraging an end.

So when I hear it,
I snark back with the rattle of a snake
searching for a leg or limb to entwine around
and wholly combine to. Anything. A tree would do.
Oh, I'd hold it to the density of stone, and squat
silently within this other being which ticks so stoically
to oppose the cicada's ferocious moon-flicking.
Inside I'd laugh a rapturous cackling laugh
as the pill bottles rattle in my arthritic hands.

Back here in the cold –
I reflect on the thoughts I have when I'm alone
and I'm boiled down to solitude, condensed into
this old stone thing, and the cicada decides to sing.

It Frays

The arachnid trickles across the pillow silk like blood might run, like licking,
as a frown moves down a face. Hooks, etched from sable,
hawk into thatched threads – tickled to fray, and
click, click, click go the coiling thorns,
mounted in preparation for a strike. A brush of air on these palps
and the giant raises on iron arches to bare a copious nut-belly –
a fortified conker bristling with arrows,
primed to prick their fire through the skin of plums, ripe to suckle on.
It is Goliath, the cotton weave his cobweb.

Then, tissued away
                released onto a landing leaf, softly softly,
                                it withers,
                                        curling shy of sunlight.

Little Shoe

It shone – a world on a little satin thing
poking through the rose of wrinkled Tyvek;
a ruby to slip a lily into.

Lifting it from the case, I sit it on one cottoned palm,
fingers fanning beneath like a lark's wing around an egg
or a teacup, stitched from sun-silk
and curving to a point slim enough to perch on
the thumb-loop of a girl
painting a sky she watched in childhood.
All her favourite garden sights;
bluebirds, tamed hoopoes, palm-swifts
in peach of blushing cheek and perching proudly
amongst trickling vines in lagoon blue.
Hosts of cloud-like lotus flowers – falling
in a white flush of doves,
swooping on the whistle-crack of wind
up from the stone floor. Scenes from before

this life of little stitches, shuffling steps on fists of flesh
in groups of golden lilies tipped with red
and held together by hands grasping sisters' sleeves.
Tied in this amorphous knot of quiet,
each face meets another mouthing the name
inked in a bird's nest of strokes
hidden inside her shoes.

Chaplin Moon

Most often this watercolour, a murky middle-mood
waiting for an anchor. Every twist, half-expecting
a bowel to squeeze down a wall, thick as clay sliding.
No warning. Just the hot punch and moth-flutters
to reassure of sex.

It does happen sometimes. Hot and rash

and the slap-dash oils are gelatinous, but I'm brighter –
tingle fingertips thankful. Rounder. Hair down. Holding
my hips like moons of Venus. A bomb no longer carried,
dropped. Job done. Congratulatory slap

but the next moon is a Chaplin-moon again, and I'm
miming, slipping-up in big boots, waiting for a punchline.
A watercolour of black, white, and a murky middle-mood.

And where then do you go?

That left-hand heap;
an artificial igloo in Christchurch, electric-berry gelato,
Poirot fingers a moustache, motorcycle maintenance, spanners,
a king and his nephews, English pageantry; retiring to Bath,

the sloping lot in the middle trashed-stack;
a ring, a sentient hall, pad thai licked from a plate,
a sword-naming ceremony, a stream, prayer flags in Nepal,
temple doors and dust, France; delirious, hot dreaming

and the spread few, open and fleshy;
a catalogue of brie, an unearthed giant,
a diamond's flaw, a moonstone, a spinal circuit board,
a car pile-up, a bouquet; rosettes, marigolds, peonies

and all the remaining loads
are places I'm yet to go, though the tickets are bought
and stored by my bedside, on the fish tank, in every room –
waiting bookbound; all set for departure.

The Raven and the Wood Pigeon

My personal prophesy shall be
the raven and the wood pigeon
drawn in the same portrait.

This is not often seen,
but why not?

Seed and rot, stalk and shine.
Are these not part
of the very same apple we all eat
from the split – when we grow teeth?

Consider the impermanence
of the fruit.

My personal prophesy shall be
a house of feathers, so soft
that the walls move when we breathe.

PART THREE

Inventions

and each bolt of lightning brightens
the sky
but only for a second –
and then it is dark again.

Looper

Be prepared for the route
through six rooms;

the first is a loft, painted in sky and the faint
grey of irises, spectacle steel, cloud-light.
Mouth-sized currants, dribbling lychee,
the kiss of steam rising from a lawn,

and then the second parts its lips. This is the black canal
that, in a swallow, squeezes a body through
rotted wood, fractured rafters. Memories come back –
snowing dried petals from buds long since bloomed.

The third is a flesh bedroom; velvet-rose cushions
plumped with goose-feathers, the soap-scent
of grandma's milky violets, and a wrinkled wink
from a man who looks like an old apple. Talcum,

crisp cotton, and a porcelain bowl – slopping
with hot water as it pours you on the fourth. It's over
in a flash. A scarlet bite and the hush of paper tearing.
Pull, rip apart the soul and bone to the wail of mother's

war-horn, the smell of an electric storm, and twilight.
The fifth and final is a tomb, loam-painted-plum
and the walls are warm, living, soft and bloody soil
moving in tides to a low hum, a song you once knew.

The sixth is the concave, dirty white of an egg
which forms around you in the long night. Sea salt crackles
on the tongue. You are *the sun* pushing to be born;
your soft nails splintering clean slate with an innocent *crack*.

A hermit crab makes his home inside a doll's head

Seated, he is a fist, and when he crawls
an open hand,
his underbelly raw as a fig's middle.
His weakness drags the sand, an immature length
born for burial. Crawl on it,
curl it into the segments of palm.
Pretend it doesn't exist. Seek.
Seek. Slowly seek

and find a sheltering place, a red womb. *Here.*
A bulbous cove to birth a safer world,
half within, and half without.
He thrusts a naked thumb inside the head
(up through the neck)
and clamps the cheek behind the teeth
with a cooling uropod, a hook with an eye for darkness.
Such a find, this ruddy pink rock.
Only a limpet or two live within, and on the skin
a pair of sky-cast barnacles watch the stars
for one last time before the deep,
the end, the beginning.

* * *

Sometimes you see a face in the rock pool.
Children hide in mother's coats, men blink and look away.
A baby's head drags across the sea bed in jolts.
Two white-cast runes, lids always open.

The Molecular Structure of Tides

It has been discovered that the molecular structure of water
contains ghosts.
History is marked in covalent bonds like notches on a bedpost,
and so an ornamental garden pond might contain a mammoth,
lashes from an Aztec Priestess, or a swan's wing –
all returned to the water from rain.
Tides are time, swept towards us.

Some ghosts will answer questions we didn't ask;
spluttering binary code onto string between two pins.
The programme is working to determine from these recordings
what to do. Musings of emperors,
philosophies of invertebrates – they will all outlast us
and the everyday devices of the past, as noted
by the superfluous dead *en masse*.
We've run out of other people to ask
and the world isn't doing too well,
all things considered.

Plant life

We're tied into carrying clusters of plants with us
at all times, like respirators, or portable dialysis machines.
'It's your civic duty', 'fulfil your O2 quota',
'here's your weekly batch of filtered water',
and with each new birthday a fresh crate of Boston ferns.
We rock around the streets like medieval milk maids
staying clear of each other, lest we bruise a root
or drop a leaf. Always a relief to reach home unscathed.

I received a spotted tiger lily last year, and a rare orchid
which I promptly overwatered, so my left lung was aborted
the following month. Confiscated organs are fed
through the composter, crafting a softer bed
for the greenest breathers to blossom in and breed further.
Now I receive half the ferns I did before, and breathe shallowly,
hardly tasting the hard-earned air at all.

Sun 2.0

Sun 2.0 doesn't warm the earth like the other model did.
Those who can remember Sun 1.0 recall an orb with an edge that curled.
You'd blind yourself to look at it, but often you couldn't help but look –
particularly towards the end.
You could tell the time by it, or map out a virtual world
by its angle to the earth. Sun 1.0 birthed flickering shadows
which brought to life mountains, trees, molehills –
all dappled like the freckled skin of a giant.
And as the day's industry diminished
your shadow would stretch – dancing longer than you.

But Sun 2.0 is an ultraviolet spread of duck-egg. Lamps light up
and dim at times democratically agreed. It refracts
through the factor block we're glazed in,
we're pork crackling, cooking down in our dermal fabric.
My skin does sting, and it itches – the finger-jig.

All the while, our shadows are stuck to their dimensions,
as static as most things, at all times alike
until night arrives, and they fade.

What we can learn from thermodynamics

Each of us can't win, even the effort of fighting works us older.

We sit in opposing bells of our hourglass.
My particles shift into your mouth until the world flips
serendipitously, and you share my particles
(now your own) back with me.

We see ourselves at the speed of light
and this is our entropy. Here – have my coat,
I'll feed it through the hole.
Take my heat, I don't mind the cold.

But this road. We've been on it before.
We can't go back to the apartment years, the parties,
the parks. We're heading for an absolute zero.
Should we stop now, stretch through the centre-fold

to touch arms, fingertips, soft plump faces, toes?
Tomorrow comes close, and each day we eat the other
until we're too weak to raise a fork, or slice a knife,
and the little that remains dissipates.

A Recipe for Meringue

In 2017, the first known attempt at creating genetically modified human embryos in the US occurred in Portland, Oregon.

Evoke the light touch required to make meringue.

Whisk the mix like you'd doctor a diary entry,
retrospectively. Deftly tap the steel spoon
to play a tune, a fine one,
and wear her shoes. Lace them up
in predetermined blue. Stick to her mother's recipe.

Avoid the starry mess of too much sugar;
drizzle it in like a snowstorm in an old film.
Be wary of the golden spider, hiding in milky white.
Seal off the windows, so rain won't haze
the sculpted peaks. This isn't crochet, or lace.

Keep true to the light touch needed to craft meringue.
Bake light, and slow. Serve on a platter,
a bald canvas for the gallery, sketched only
with a mosaic-fingerprint, marking cracks
through which tangs rise after a rain dance.

The Issue of the Day

It has been discovered that what's known of the fifth fundamental force
is the trace of the thing itself. The target has the intrinsic ability
to evolve away from its common design into something
that cannot be judged, measured, or predicted.
It's as if this force has anticipated the immediate
and acted prior to arrival. The *smallest shift*, moving
in simultaneous alignment with its own phantom.

Researchers have tried to evaluate its purpose for years
but remain vague, and every time they're on the news
they look younger.

The Wire

It's wonderful, this Wire.
At the switch, I slow into macro
to reach you. We're all just particles,
and the *need to be there quickly.*

But still –
something doesn't seem… *right.*
We all share a feeling
that we were different then,
and then, and then;

and whispers spread
that each time we share the Wire,
we're changed,
and passing on the genetic code
of folk we don't know.

That our children are not our children
but the mass parturition
of unclean programming.
All the same and yet none familiar.

Mnemosyne

My new *Innovative Tongue* converts words
into Officon, Afrikaans, Mandarin,
Japanese, Spanish and all the Sirius tributaries
and can be reprogrammed on the move.
A modest download is all that's needed,
an invoice, then reset.

It can elucidate a thousand thoughts
into one poignant line, with a dead-on dialect
to bring gods to tears.
It can coil around a throat
or mend with a curing hum.
It censors my swearing, when necessary.

But I am losing the words for flavours.
Bacon, and cream, and the mellow tang of strawberries.
Now they don't taste of anything.

Taxes

After she checked herself in,
found her cubicle, stripped
from gaunt thins into surgical linens
and awaited the anaesthetist on duty –
she thought back to her grandmother.

The roundedness of her, an entire Earth;
scarred pink from numerous Benidorm afternoons
and boastful flesh; *full of herself*,
pruned into a cognisant topiary.
Never owing anything to the state, she'd give you
the back of her hand rather than a share of liver,
an eye, or her eustachian tube;
and it would still mean something to you.

Her body failed her in the end, naturally,
occupied by fostered carcinogens from her little choices.
Her world demanded no court-orders,
carving up the cadaver-in-arrears,
or an official apology for her lifestyle.

From my point of view

So this is home, then; singled off
and sectioned, hair in threads
and skin turning in, form-folded
on innocent hinges? I see my life's philosophy
engraved on my parts. There's my conduction rate,
and an actuator's sparks –
sharp and blue beneath the striplights.

These ones, dressed in bleach-white,
asked one another if it would hurt
when they cut out my tongue.
None guessed the answer.
Instead, they packed my mouth with dirt
and foam, then in quiet tones;
waste not, want not.
But you see – that tongue was mine,
plaited down my throat
and roped around my larynx.
They couldn't have taken more of me.

These ones, smelling of garlic, cared
about my falling hair. This care is fractured.
I laid for days before my dress
was dissolved by the acid bath,
the emergent me all fleshy red.
They numbered each follicle before converging
over fussy bits like fingernails,
nostrils, the rivers of blue wrist tattoos –
giving my skin a score.

I'm feeling lighter all the time.
Maybe it's the excess of arrows on boxes
always pointing down, like mad sprigs
determined to grow. They should face up,
towards the light, but how would I know
what's right for a room stacked with coffins
and broken limbs.

And now –
though they didn't like their brownness
before, they've marked out my eyes
for another head. Perhaps I'll see again
from a different height?
My peripherals travel so weary and slow,
each thought motionless in the air
like a hoverfly, something still, but alive,
or a glass singing, close to its shatter
and stop.

Something, Not Nothing

No, no, you're wrong.
Your horizon flicks by, *a film*,
and any stoking of our lives is proven
by observing our hands stirring it,
our selves; the spoon.

See it another way.

The flowers bloom, *through your eye.*
The grass is a maelstrom, a portrait of a field.
Touch is the supposition of a full-tongue-lick
and tingles are concepts.

What is nothing?
I've heard it before,
but your nothing is cupped by a cockle-shell;
an outside looking in, birthing its shape.
An empty cup is a cup.

And blanks that sit side by side
as isolated entities, you ask?
Nothings, no-ones.
How are you perceiving them to be apart
unless one bears more weight than the other?
A void in solitary is something too,
in its conceiving *you're gifting it a price.*
Infusing by thinking, manifesting meaning
into vacuums, all rooms, filling stillness.

So this isn't nothing. Don't be sorry.
There's no such thing.

Knitting Needles

She picks up the needles
to prove that old string
is also a blossoming web of tight knots –
only unravelled, sleeping in an armchair.

She smiles at the frays,
the twists in the melody.

Dropped stitches can be as comely as lace
when they're remembered,
and each tied-off end
is a beginning.

Questioning the human branch

They're lucky to be here in their short lifetimes –
posing on the mirror between day and night,

a tumble of stick-things convinced they're steel, pressing elbows
on the water that carries their shadows out of sight.

Above their crowns, a wall of yellow-stones is butter warm
and the clouds don't yet shiver from the death of light.

The flock doesn't flinch the day the grey towers crumble
into pigeon feathers, and substance comes second to height –

but they should question this branch. Why do they rest in the road
when the roar comes – blinded by the moon's white

and smiling under rubber? When sleeping, do they forget that
they can't see in the dark or save the dreams they lock up tight?

How can we be different? Is it always inside of us, then,
this ending we greet as if everything is alright?

Endnotes

A Portrait on a House-Skin

Living in South Africa and Zimbabwe, the Ndebeles are renowned for their artistic talents, especially when it comes to their painted houses.

Glyptodon Terraces

Glyptodons were large, heavily armoured mammals that lived during the Pleistocene epoch and co-existed with humans. They were roughly the same size and weight as Volkswagen Beetles, and were hunted for their shells.

Pterosaur

Mary Anning was an English fossil collector, dealer, and palaeontologist in the nineteenth century who became world famous for the historic finds she made in Jurassic marine fossil beds in the cliffs along the English Channel. She is known for discovering several important fossils, including the first pterosaur fossil found in the British Isles.

Coprolites are fossilised faeces of animals that lived millions of years ago.

Libulan reads the sage smoke for an answer

In Filipino mythology, Libulan is frequently portrayed as a man or a woman, or a 'two spirit' divinity. A deity of the moon, farming, and fertility, softly-spoken Libulan was revered for prophesies and shaman-like abilities.

Siddhārtha hears a song performed by a travelling musician

When Siddhārtha was born in Ancient Nepal, a prophesy dictated that he would either become the king of the whole world or a holy man. To shelter him from suffering and lead him towards kingship, his father engineered a perfect world for him to live in. At 29, Siddhārtha made his own choice to leave the palace. After years of inner searching, he became the Buddha.

Yaśodharā was the wife of Prince Siddhārtha before he left the palace to seek enlightenment. Only seven days before he started out alone, Yaśodharā had given birth to their son. Years later, she became a fully ordained female monastic.

Ahalya

In Hindu mythology, Ahalya is the wife of the sage Gautama Maharishi. Many Hindu scriptures say that she was seduced by Indra (the king of gods), cursed by her husband for infidelity, and liberated from the curse by Rama.

Mynah birds originate from Africa, India, and south east Asia and are known for their ability to mimic sounds. They are lively, social, and as young birds they are easily tamed.

Gloria, Hag

Originating in ancient Europe as a Celtic fire festival, Samhain marks the end of the harvest and the beginning of winter. In the Druid tradition, Samhain celebrates the dead with a festival on 31st October and often features communion with the dead.

The Morrígan Meets a Lover on the Battlefield

The Morrígan is an old Irish Goddess associated with war, fate, and foretelling doom, death or victory in battle.

Bean-Nighe

In Scottish folklore, the bean-nighe is a spirit regarded as an omen of death and a messenger from the Otherworld. She is a type of ban-sìth that haunts desolate, remote streams and washes the clothing of those about to die.

On Opening a Love Note Delivered by Snail

Mycelium is the foundation of a mushroom. When a spore comes into contact with an underlayer in the right environment and condition, germination occurs. This is the birth of mycelium.

The main body of most fungi is made up of fine threads called hyphae. Each fungus will have vast numbers of these hyphae, all tangling to make up the web known as mycelium.

Sun Burn

Toxoplasmosis is a disease transmitted through undercooked meat, soil, or in cat faecal matter.

Little Shoe

This poem was written after a day working in museum conservation. I'd come across a tiny pair of shoes that belonged to a woman in 1800s China whose feet had been bound at a young age.

Tyvek is a material used in museum stores to conserve and protect historical artefacts.

Chaplin Moon

Polycystic ovary syndrome is a condition that affects how the ovaries work. Symptoms often include irregular cycles (or no cycles at all), heavy periods, difficulty conceiving, and weight gain.

Mnemosyne

A figure from Greek mythology, Mnemosyne was the Titan goddess of memory and remembrance and the architect of language and words.

Taxes

Eustachian tubes are the small tubes that run between your middle ears and the upper throat and are responsible for regulating ear pressure.

Acknowledgements

Firstly, I have to thank Jamie McGarry for believing in me and my poetry enough to publish my second collection and first full-length book of poetry. You're an absolute star, and I can't imagine a better (or more cheeky) editor or publisher to work with.

Secondly, I have to thank Jo Brandon for being the wisest and most considerate poetry editor I could've been matched with. Always full of passion and curiosity, you managed to make me see my words in a new light, and I couldn't have done it without you.

Thirdly, a thank you to Russell Jones for reading these poems multiple times and guiding me every step of the way. Thank you to Ben Hardaker, for (again) illustrating my poetry in such a unique and understanding way. A big thank you to Charlotte Marlow, for inspiring me to write about women in mythology (and opening up a whole other can of worms). I'll chuck in a thank you to my agent too, Ed Wilson, for standing by during all my authoring endeavours and being a relentless ball of enthusiastic energy. I appreciate it, Ed.

Thanks also to *Magma*, *The Linnet's Wings*, *The Lake*, *The Writer's Café*, *The Emma Press*, *Platypus Press*, *Shoreline of Infinity*, *Bonnie's Crew*, *Runcible Spoon*, *Mookychick Books*, *Riggwelter*, *The Interpreter's House*, *Amaryllis*, *Three Drops Press*, *Ink, Sweat, & Tears*, *The Fat Damsel*, *Dragon Yaffle*, *Eyewear Publishing*, and *I am Not a Silent Poet*, who published some of these poems for the first time. Thank you to Medusa Collective too, for producing some of these poems as incredible art songs, ready to set the operatic world on fire.

And finally, thank you to everyone who has ever listened to me talk about poetry or said something nice about these wee lyrical stories. Everything you do or say, no matter how small, spurs me on and encourages me to keep learning and finding new ways to collaborate and grow.